James Williams

SOLO PIANO

SECOND FLOOR MUSIC

Exclusively Distributed By

HAL•LEONARD™
CORPORATION

7777 W. Bluemound Rd. P.O. Box 13819 Milwaukee, WI 53213

ISBN 0-7935-3256-6

Compositions and arrangements by *James Williams*
Edited by *Pamela Baskin Watson*
Photographs by *Jimmy Katz*, Giant Steps
Music typography by *Osho Endo*
Book design by *Maureen Sickler*
A Don Sickler Production

James Williams
ARRANGEMENTS FOR SOLO PIANO

*Dedicated to
the memory of my mother,
whose wisdom and vision are with me
in every facet of my life.*

Mrs. Louise E. Williams
October 19, 1914–January 30, 1992

"**M**usic has been the common denominator in making friends and in seeing places that I thought I'd only read about while growing up in Memphis. Most of all, it has given me the privilege of extending the great traditions of Louis Armstrong, Duke Ellington, Count Basie, Thelonious Monk, Charlie Parker, Sarah Vaughan, and others." Pianist and composer James Williams has added his own distinctive style to the musical legacies of his inspirations. The compositions in this piano folio display his trademark sound that has garnered the praise of musicians, critics, and fans worldwide.

James Williams was born in Memphis, Tennessee, on March 8, 1951. He began taking piano lessons at the age of 13, and gained his earliest professional experience playing gospel and rhythm and blues gigs around his hometown. While attending Memphis State University, he began to cultivate and expand his interest in jazz. Williams led a combo that placed first in the National Collegiate Jazz Festival two times. The group subsequently performed at the Newport Jazz Festival in New York City, and at the Kennedy Center in Washington, D.C.

Williams received his degree in music education from Memphis State in 1974. A few months later, he joined the faculty of the Berklee College of Music in Boston. While in Boston, Williams furthered his own musical education by performing regularly with musicians such as Sonny Stitt, Joe Henderson, Woody Shaw, Thad Jones, Clark Terry, Chet Baker, Milt Jackson, and Red Norvo. In addition, his work at Berklee gave him ample opportunity to develop his composing skills, and brought him into contact with such eminent jazz composers as Charles Mingus.

In 1977, Williams joined Art Blakey's Jazz Messengers, becoming the first of three Memphians to hold the piano chair in that group (Donald Brown and Mulgrew Miller followed Williams into the band). Williams stayed with Blakey for four years, logging countless hours on the road, and recording nine albums. Like Horace Silver, Cedar Walton, Bobby Timmons, and the other great Messengers pianists before him, Williams was a frequent contributor to the Messengers' book of exciting, original compositions. From 1979 to 1981, he was part of a now-famous Messengers lineup that included saxophonists Bill Pierce and Bobby Watson, bassist Charles Fambrough, and trumpeter Wynton Marsalis. That unit garnered a Grammy Award nomination for the album *Straight Ahead* (Concord).

Williams released his first album as a leader in 1978, and has since recorded in a variety of settings, including duos, trios, quartets, and sextets. Most recently, he has been musical director of the Contemporary Piano Ensemble, which includes Donald Brown, Harold Mabern, Mulgrew Miller, Geoff Keezer, bassist Christian McBride, and drummer Tony Reedus. After the January 1994 release of "The Key Players" (CBS / Sony), the Ensemble embarked on a 21-city tour of the United States from February 2 to March 6. In 1992, he recorded *James Williams Meets The Saxophone Masters* (DIW / Columbia), which features George Coleman, Joe Henderson, and Billy Pierce. Some of his most successful recordings have been the *Magical Trio* series on EmArcy, which feature Williams with a veteran bassist and drummer, such as Ray Brown and Art Blakey or Elvin Jones. In addition, Williams has served as a producer for Sunnyside Communications, overseeing record dates for Bill Pierce, saxophonist Bill Easley, and Donald Brown. Most of the material in this folio is derived from a pair of Williams' sextet dates, *Alter Ego* and *Progress Report*, recorded for Sunnyside in 1984 and 1985, respectively.

Since moving to New York from Boston in 1984, Williams has been in constant demand as a sideman. While continuing to perform and record as a leader, he has also appeared in New York with Milt Jackson, Tal Farlow, Art Farmer, Elvin Jones, Freddie Hubbard, and Slide Hampton, to name just a few. Williams has continued his educational involvement by working frequently as a clinician at workshops and jazz festivals across the country. In 1988 and 1992, he was artist-in-residence at Harvard University and Dartmouth College, respectively, and from 1984 to 1985, he was a visiting instructor in the jazz program at Hartt College of the University of Hartford. For Williams, educating others in the jazz tradition is an enjoyable responsibility: "Lending a hand to youngsters helps extend the music itself. I've realized you have to put things back and keep rejuvenating."

James Williams continues to expand and share his knowledge and understanding of jazz through his compositions. The pianist who studies the arrangements contained in this volume will find them to be as deeply rooted in the jazz tradition as they are challenging, innovative, and imaginative.

JAMES WILLIAMS ON RECORDINGS

AS LEADER:

Flying Colors *Zim ZMS 2005 (1978)*
Everything I Love *Concord Jazz CJ 104 (1979)*
Images (Of Things To Come) *Concord Jazz CJ 140 (1981)*
The Arioso Touch *Concord Jazz CJ 192 (1982)*
Alter Ego* *Sunnyside Communications SSC 1007 (1984)*
Progress Report* *Sunnyside Communications SSC 1012 (1985)*
Magical Trio 1* *EmArcy (Polygram) 832 859-1 (1988)*
Magical Trio 2 *EmArcy (Nippon Phonogram) 20PJ 10120 (1988)*
Meet The Magical Trio *EmArcy (Polygram) EJD-4 (1989)*
Four Pianos For Phineas* *Toshiba TOCJ 5528 (1990)*
Attitude Of An Everyday Man *Toshiba-EMI TOCJ-5741 (1992)*
James Williams Meets The Saxophone Masters *DIW-Columbia CK 53430 (1993)*
The Key Players (Contemporary Piano Ensemble)* *CBS (1994)*
Up To The Minute Blues* *CBS (1994)*

AS CO-LEADER:

JAMES WILLIAMS / RICHARD DAVIS / RONNIE BURRAGE
I Remember Clifford *DIW DIW-601 (1990)*

JAMES WILLIAMS / DENNIS IRWIN
Focus *Red VPA 132 (1978)*

JAMES WILLIAMS / EMIL VICKLICKY
Together / Spolu *Supraphon 1115 3013 H (1982)*

JAMES WILLIAMS TRIO / BOYS' CHOIR OF HARLEM
Christmas Carols & Sacred Songs* *Toshiba / Blue Note 5647 (1991)*

JAMES WILLIAMS and others
Memphis Piano Convention *DIW DIW-613 (1993)*

JAMES WILLIAMS and others
Memphis Convention *DIW DIW-874 (1993)*

AS SIDEMAN:

with ART BLAKEY AND THE JAZZ MESSENGERS
In My Prime, Vol. 1 *Timeless SJP 114 (1978)*
In This Korner *Concord Jazz CJ 68 (1978)*
In My Prime, Vol. 2 *Timeless SJP 118 (1979)*
Reflections In Blue *Timeless SJP 128 (1979)*
Live At Montreux And Northsea *Timeless SJP 150 (1981)*
Straight Ahead *Concord Jazz CJ 168 (1981)*
Album Of The Year *Timeless SJP 155 (1981)*
Live At Bubba's *Who's Who In Jazz WWLP 21019 (1981)*
Art Blakey In Sweden *Amigo AMLP 839 (1982)*
The Best Of Art Blakey *Concord Jazz 4495 (1992)*

with TAL FARLOW
Cookin' On All Burners *Concord Jazz CJ 204 (1982)*
The Best Of Art Blakey *Concord Jazz CJ 4495 (1992)*

with ART FARMER
Something To Live For *Contemporary C 14029 (1987)*
Blame It On My Youth *Contemporary C 14042 (1988)*
Ph.D. *Contemporary CCD 14055 2 (1989)*

with CURTIS FULLER / PEPPER ADAMS
Four On The Outside *Timeless SJP 124 (1978)*

with TOM HARRELL
Sail Away *Contemporary 14054 (1990)*

with MICHELE HENDRICKS
Me And My Shadow *Muse MCD 5404 (1990)*

with RICHARD HOLLYDAY
Moment's Notice *Shiah SR 114 (1983)*

with JAVON JACKSON
Me And Mr. Jones *Criss Cross 1053 (1992)*

with PETER LEITCH
Portraits And Dedications *Criss Cross 1039 (1990)*

with PHINEAS NEWBORN
I've Something To Say* *EmArcy 20PJ-10148 (1988)*

with BILLY PIERCE
William The Conqueror* *Sunnyside Communications SSC 1013 (1985)*

with EMILY REMLER
Take Two *Concord Jazz CJ 195 (1982)*

with MARVIN "Smitty" SMITH
The Road Less Traveled *Concord Jazz CJ 379 (1989)*

with JACK WALRATH
Master Of Suspense *Blue Note BLJ 46905 (1987)*
Neohippus *Blue Note CDP7 91101 2 (1989)*

with SADAO WATANABE
Parker's Mood *Elektra 9 60475-1 (1985)*

with BOBBY WATSON
All Because Of You *Roulette SR 5010 (1978)*
Tailor Made *Columbia CK 53416 (1993)*

with JOE WILDER
Alone With Just My Dreams *Evening Star ES-101 (1991)*

with RICKEY WOODARD
Tokyo Express *Candid 79527 (1993)*

* Also produced by James Williams

This composition was first recorded on ALTER EGO/ James Williams (Sunnyside SSC 1007)

A Touching Affair

JAMES WILLIAMS

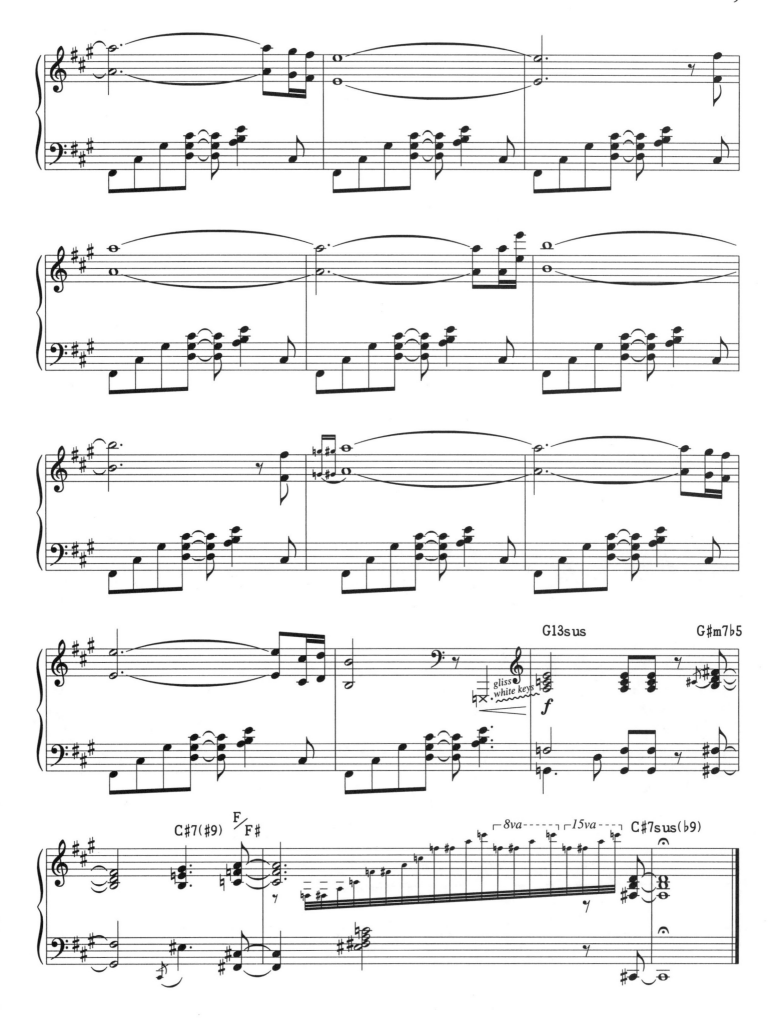

This composition was first recorded on EVERYTHING I LOVE/ James Williams (Concord CJ-104)

For My Nephews

Medium swing (♩ = *ca.* 110)

JAMES WILLIAMS

* eighth notes: 9/8 feel

This composition was first recorded on ALTER EGO/ James Williams (Sunnyside SSC 1007)

Black Scholars

Medium up swing ($\quarternote$ = *ca.* 210)

JAMES WILLIAMS

This composition was first recorded on PROGRESS REPORT / James Williams (Sunnyside SSC 1012)

Mr. Day's Dream

JAMES WILLIAMS

Medium swing (♩ = *ca.* 106)

This composition was first recorded on ALTER EGO/ James Williams (Sunnyside SSC 1007)

Fourplay

JAMES WILLIAMS

This composition was first recorded on PROGRESS REPORT / James Williams (Sunnyside SSC 1012)

Renaissance Lovers

JAMES WILLIAMS

This composition was first recorded on IMAGES (OF THINGS TO COME) / James Williams (Concord CJ-140)

Images (Of Things To Come)

Medium swing (♩ = *ca.* 108)

JAMES WILLIAMS

This composition was first recorded on FLYING COLORS/ James Williams (Zim Records ZMS-200)

The Changing Of The Guard*

JAMES WILLIAMS

Uptempo swing (♩ = *ca.* 240)

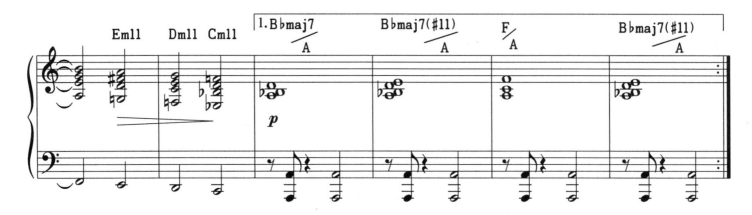

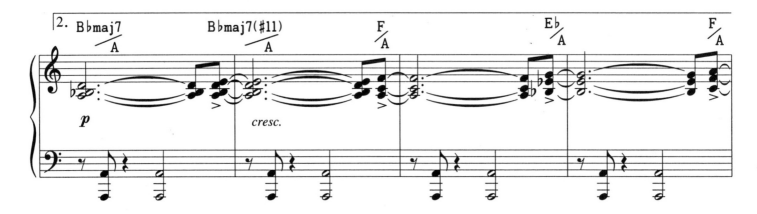

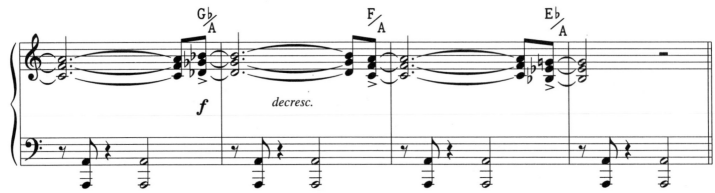

* First recorded as "1977 A.D.", this composition is dedicated to drummer Alan Dawson.

The Lovers' Celebration

JAMES WILLIAMS

This composition was first recorded on ALTER EGO/ James Williams (Sunnyside SSC 1007)

Alter Ego

Medium Latin (♩ = *ca.* 104)

JAMES WILLIAMS

This composition was first recorded on THE ARIOSO TOUCH/ James Williams (Concord Jazz CJ-192)

Arioso

JAMES WILLIAMS

First recorded on PROGRESS REPORT / James Williams (Sunnyside SSC 1012)

Progress Report

Uptempo swing (♩ = *ca.* 252)

JAMES WILLIAMS

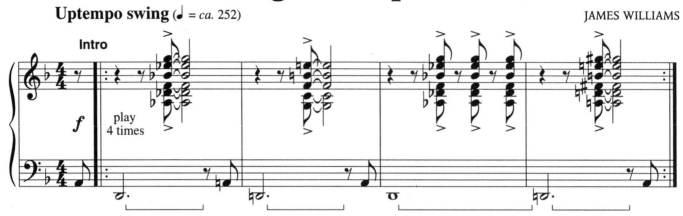

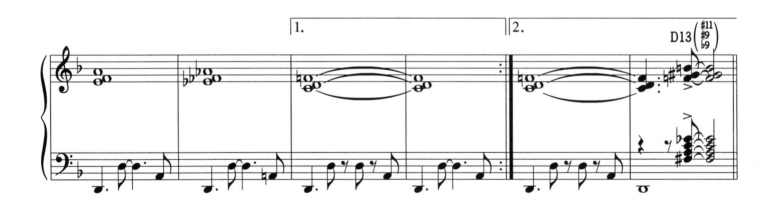

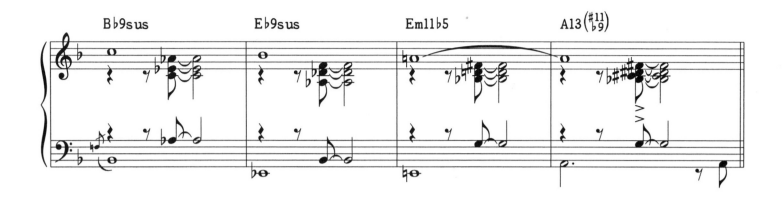

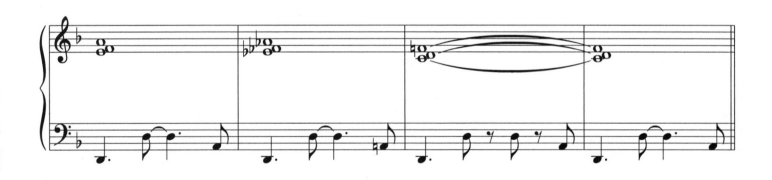

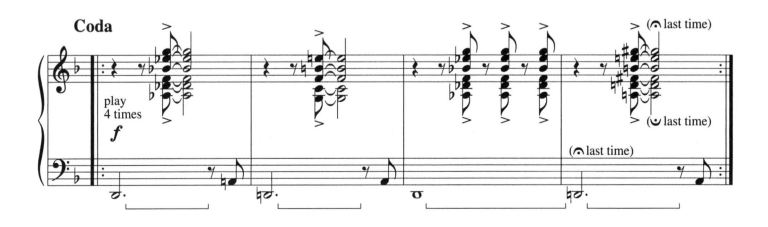

This composition was first recorded on ALTER EGO/ James Williams (Sunnyside SSC 1007)

Beauty Within

JAMES WILLIAMS